Art Media Series

Creating with Clay

Lothar Kampmann

VNR Van Nostrand Reinhold Company/New York

Illustrations
Illustrations in the first part of this book came from the Ruhr Training College for Elementary Teachers, Dortmund section, and from the author. Those in the Appendix show children's work from the art classes of Overberg School, Recklinghausen, and others are by Wilhelm Hohmann, Recklinghausen. The illustrations of the Greek amphora and the Chinese jug are from the Holle Picture Archives, Wiesbaden. The impression of the Babylonian cylindrical seal is taken from *Typos*, by Ben Rosen, published by Otto Maier Verlag, Ravensburg, and we thank Rosenthal AG for the composition of the illustrations on p. 37.

The firm of Conrad Naber, Lilienthal near Bremen, kindly placed at our disposal the Model M20/S kiln.

Sponsored by the Günther Wagner Pelikan-Werke, Hannover; and Koh-I-Nor, Inc., 100 North Street, Bloomsbury, New Jersey 08804.

Impression of a Babylonian cylindrical Seal.

Geometrical grave amphora, Greece, eighth century BC.

In the earliest records of mankind, in which modern man seeks solutions to the puzzles of the past, the theme is often of clay, earth and mud, materials which can be kneaded and which were the very first to be formed and shaped by primitive man. In his hands the shapeless clay was to transform, according to his taste and will, into lasting utensils and objects to serve new purposes, for building and for cultural ends.

We would have known little or nothing of these lost cultures, were it not for the work of the archaeologists, who have dug up clay tablets and pottery from long-forgotten centuries and made them available to the world. Babylonian clay writing tablets have survived, if only in fragments, and they tell the expert the story of mankind, its customs, cares, needs and pleasures, from before the era of writing.

The arts of decoration and ornament appear at a very early period, sometimes coarse and primitive, at other times of amazingly delicate artistry. Such utensils and figures tell us that man's need was never only to eat, drink and survive. He decorated his dwellings, his possessions and himself, for his own pleasure or to honour his gods. The ornamental arts stood at the birth of all civilizations.

Over the centuries man's mastery over materials increased. He learned quickly how to refine and classify it so that different raw materials for differing purposes were at his command, and the technical and artistic treatment became ever more assured and refined.

One community would learn from others, and no one knows with certainty where it all began. Egypt taught the West, among many other things, the art of molten glass and of glazing. The ancient Greeks discovered a special type of black paint, which, like the Roman *terra sigilata* still proves an insoluble puzzle to the modern ceramic laboratory.

Faïence and majolica became world-renowned, and Walter von Tschirnhaus and the 'Goldmaker', Johann Friedrich Böttger, rediscovered for the West the Chinese porcelain which till then had been as valuable as gold.

We cannot now imagine our world without the products of these primitive basic materials. Like ancient man, children today can instinctively shape and mould plastic materials according to their own tastes and ideas. But in the meantime, new substances which can be kneaded and shaped have been developed, apart from potter's clay, and suited to the requirements of home and school. These, as well as clay, will be discussed in the following pages.

Chinese jug decorated with flat incised peonies China (Ting-yao).

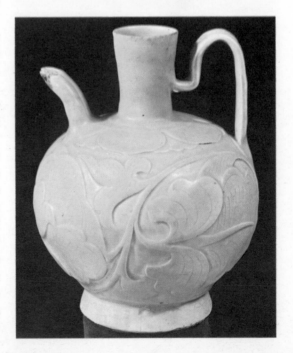

4

PLASTIC MATERIALS IN CHILDREN'S HANDS

Through the sense of touch we experience most intensely the objects of our world, for in touch we have the closest, most intimate contact. Touching, grasping, kneading, together with seeing, thinking and testing, make up modelling. The whole body is involved. Through grasping things, young babies gain their first impressions and lasting experiences. But their hands are trained, much too quickly, to use specialized tools, despite the fact that Nature has obviously designed them for manifold activities. The modern way of life, with its continual improvements in technology, is robbing human hands of one manual skill after another. They and their crafts are no longer required: they revert to their simplest duty as mere carriers, and tend to become clumsy and unskilled. Through contact with plastic materials the hand can be taught and trained, made sensitive and responsive, and led on from the simplest forms of handling to skilful manipulation.

All small children enjoy helping mother when she is baking, and not merely for the titbits. They see, and copy her when she kneads and rolls out the dough for biscuits and pies, and it is the same instinct which induces the child to play with sand and clay: it fulfils their natural, healthy desire

to touch and feel. For the small child, kneading is as important as scribbling and dabbling with paints. There are three important elements in kneading and modelling: the sensuous pleasure in moulding with the hands, insight into the types and behaviour of different materials, and introduction to form and space. In modelling the child learns much about himself, his own skills and abilities, and the things which the world has to offer. He experiences in his own actions the limits of his subject. But such thought and skill cannot be taken for granted, they do not just occur of their own accord: they have to be learned, just as the arts of seeing and of touch.

A child's earliest essays at grasping are followed by kneading, and here he may make his first painful acquaintance with the resistance of a hard, unyielding object. But if his hand meets soft, plastic substance, then, without knowing it, he gets his very first experience of modelling, and just from the squeeze of a hand, some thing becomes a new thing.

We form and shape many things and our activities leave many kinds of legacies and traces, of which thousands are of no consequence. Only that which eye, hand and feeling have co-ordinated is of any worth.

Plastic materials tempt the hand to mould, and offer the right consistency for it: soft enough to be shaped by hand pressure, yet rigid and firm enough to remain in that shape as long as is desired. The ideas behind 'two-handed painting' are realized in kneading and modelling, in which both hands are used equally.

Modelling knows no age limit, but its requirements and the choice of materials will vary. In the following pages suggestions will be given for all age groups.

6

There is no need here to discuss at any length the simplest forms of kneading, done without method and instruction. We all recognize these elementary products of the child's hand. They are the beginning and foundation, and depend on no special material. Suffice to say that in every child there is the wish to use his hands, and from his parents he must get the chance to fulfil it.

The basic raw material

Many substances can be kneaded and moulded – for instance, pastry – and most mothers and children have had unpleasant experiences with congealed tar, but not all are suited to school, home and play. The easiest to obtain commercially is clay, from brickworks or potteries. It is available in many types, each with its own special qualities. It can be fine- or coarse-grained, and when baked, can be yellow, red, white, or brown, right through to black. In the second half of this book we shall go into more detail (see p.38) but in the following chapter we shall refer only to ready-to-use, kneadable clay.

Nature also provided the second material: beeswax. Among the ancient sculptors it stood in high esteem, and even today it is essential for bronze sculpture, though beeswax has given way to artificial wax. Special kneading wax has been developed for school use.

In the quest for artificial substitutes for these natural substances, which have certain drawbacks – (clay dries too quickly, and wax softens in the sun) papier-mâché has been developed. For this, coarse, unglazed paper is torn up very small and kneaded with glue or sizing. Adding powdered clay gives it finer consistency and better plasticity. It is still used for puppet heads.

A much superior development of this is a new artificial modelling material which combines the properties of papier-mâché and of potter's clay. A brand imported from Germany is Tonal, and there are various similar American products, such as Celluclay. It can be shaped like clay, dried like clay without shrinking too much, and is as unbreakable as hardened papier-mâché. This paper-clay can be sawn, filed, bored and cut like wood. It is available, like the other materials mentioned in this book, in art-supply stores.

Finally there is plasticine. This has the same plastic qualities as potter's clay, beeswax or plasticine, and like the latter is obtainable in several colours. It has the special advantage that it does not lose its plasticity. This, and its colouring, make it an ideal medium for modelling at home, in school or kindergarten.

Plastic play in sand

We are going to do as children do and start right from the beginning, and like them, get our first experiences in the sandbox. Damp sand is easiest to shape, and with it we can build, or use a negative impression made in it as a mould from which to make a positive.

We can press a hand into damp sand and leave a print, into which we pour liquid plaster of Paris, which when dry will give us a true reproduction of the hand. In the same way, using a finger or an implement — stick, pencil, etc., we can make negative shapes and fill them with plaster.

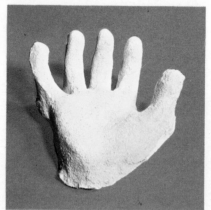

In this book we shall often refer to plaster, and certain precautions are necessary:

1. Plaster must always be stored in a dry place.
2. Plaster should only be made up in plastic or rubber vessels.
3. Plaster is always added to the water, and never the other way around.
4. Wet, well-mixed plaster should flow like thick glue or cream. But don't worry! What looked so soft and liquid often becomes hard much too quickly.
5. The plaster residue left in the container should not be washed down the sink. If this is done don't be surprised if the waste-pipe becomes blocked. Let the plaster dry and then it can easily be knocked out.
6. Plaster doesn't belong on the floor: it will quickly be tracked through the whole house.

From sand to plasticine

Now at last we come to real kneading, and what children's hands can achieve with it: making balls, cubes, 'sausages', patting or rolling out pancakes with a bottle, kneading a lump, cutting pieces from it and sticking them back again. These are elementary exercises: shaping, reshaping, taking away, adding. In one form or another we meet these constantly. For very young school infants little balls of coloured plasticine

can mean anything: apples, plums, cherries, grapes.

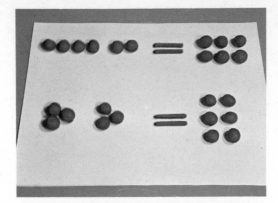

With balls they can count and do sums.

And one can illustrate the principle of relative size.

Little men and all sorts of animals can be made with plasticine or clay, with small sticks, matches and feathers as useful adjuncts.

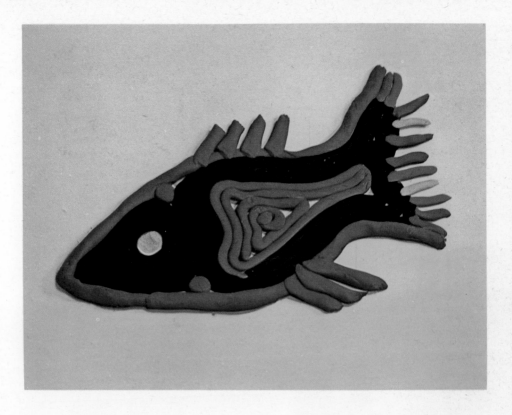

With long thin rolls of coloured clay on a flat surface we can make pictures. Balls and strips can be decorated by curving and impressing with a pencil, with the edge of a ruler, and simply with a finger.

Various 'building materials'

By pressing and rolling, we can form, apart from the strip and the sphere, the cylinder, cone and pyramid, and have at our disposal a full range of building materials. Or we can make 'building bricks' with which to build after the fashion of a mason. With plasticine the little bricks only need to be pressed into shape, but the buildings created from them will not retain their form for long.

With clay the children can play at being real masons, if between the bricks a 'mortar' is used. This consists of a mud made with clay and water (known as 'slip' in pottery). Clay buildings, however, are quickly dry and then easily broken, but paper-clay, the material mentioned earlier, that combines the properties of clay and papier-mâché, is quite strong when dry. With paper-clay bricks one can build on to the dried walls, but it is as well, before adding the new bricks, to immerse the building briefly in water.

So far it has been elementary play with simple blocks, but it should not remain so. The intention is to engage the artistic proclivities of older children, and even of adults.

Making relief patterns

We turn now to the next elementary form: the flattened disc, on which one can make relief patterns with a finger.

Now we make use of other implements, such as pencils, modelling stick, knifepoint, and everyday objects like scissors, keys, screws etc., which when pressed into the clay will leave clear impressions.

If one has old lino-cuts from which enough copies have been taken, these too can be used for stamping out patterns.

Here it is as well to mention the fact that all pictures in clay or paper-clay can of course be elaborated and decorated. It is advisable to bake ('fire') clay objects, which will acquire an attractive red appearance in the process. They can also be painted and glazed. For the elementary technique of firing and glazing see p.43.

The above applies also to paper-clay, except that this cannot be glazed. But it is possible to paint it with paper-clay 'slip' (liquid mud) tinted with water colours, or to cover it with poster paints.

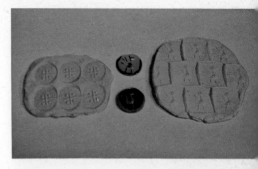

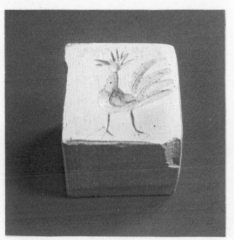

Objects thus treated can then be coated with a clear varnish, which gives the colours a special lustre, and makes them more easily handled. With relief work in paper-clay, there is another possible treatment in inlay or marquetry.

For this the relief is left to dry and then the depressed parts are filled with paper-clay of another colour. The whole plaque is dry after a time and can be smoothed down with sandpaper and polished to a high gloss with a bone or a paperknife (see p.14, lower right). With lino-cuts, as we have seen, we can produce seal reliefs. This technique is of great antiquity, and even up to the present day has never lost its appeal. We make our seal out of plaster, and the simplest way of doing this is to fill a matchbox or similar small box with liquid plaster of Paris, let it dry hard, and then scratch the motif with a knife point or lino-cutting chisel. With such seals or stamps, especially when carried out in

15

various sizes and patterns, tiled and other flat surfaces can be decorated with repeat patterns.

From Babylon comes the cylindrical seal, and we can reproduce it here. For this, liquid plaster is poured into a cardboard roll set on a tray of plasticine so that the plaster cannot seep away. When the plaster is dry the cardboard roll is removed and the resulting plaster cylinder is decorated all around with incised ornament. It is then rolled across long rectangular flat strips of clay, paperclay or plasticine, leaving patterns which can be repeated infinitely.

Creating with flat strips

The possibilities of using flat strips as a foundation for further work are not yet exhausted, and a next step might be to make a small box. The sides and bottom of the box are cut out from pieces of the same thickness. When setting the pieces together, remember to cement them with 'slip' and press all the parts firmly together.

It will be noticed that in the drying, cracks appear and that the parts spring apart. This is usually a sign that the work has not been done accurately enough or that strips of unequal thickness or dampness have been put together. The box will have a better chance of stability if all the pieces

are cut from the same strip, but it is, of course, considerably more difficult to construct a sharp-edged, angular object.

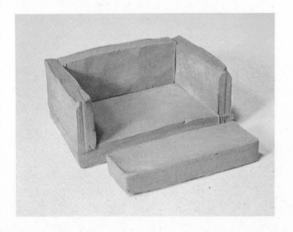

16

This problem has already been mentioned several times. Compound clay objects must be joined with the 'slip' and pressed firmly together if they are to remain whole in the drying and firing. All joints are well coated with a finger or modelling stick, and this procedure is very important. It is a necessary part of the technique, which even the greatest artist cannot shrug off. It must be practised so that the pupil does it naturally and without thinking,

otherwise it may happen that a model of especial value to him will be ruined. But such practice should not remain just a mechanical exercise. It can be the basis for a wide variety of lessons in shaping and modelling, in joining and creating hollow structures from cut clay or paper-clay.

In rolling tubes from flat strips, a lot is learned which will later prove useful in the making of hollow ware.

The combined use of the sphere, cylinder, pipe and flat strip will give much wider scope in the objects produced, and, if in clay, will lead on to the arts of glazing and firing.

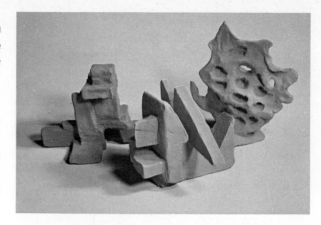

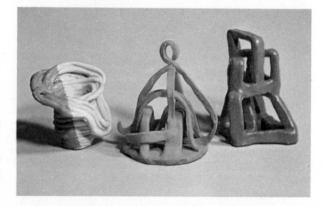

The change from exercises to creating small objects is not difficult, but do not let the child be satisfied modelling nothing but little men and other cliché figures, for inspiration and fantasy are quickly quenched. Since children of up to ten years of age have not yet grown out of the toy shop and doll's house stage they know how to put together their small worlds, and thereby gain all sorts of insights into the events and relationships of everyday things. The simple sphere, cone and square are soon forgotten; free modelling takes its place and for such work all plastic materials are to hand.
But let us return again to the

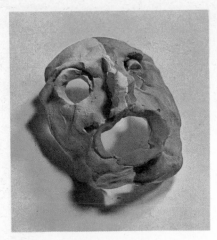

simple flat strip, which by rolling, cutting up and piecing together can be given so many forms. Clay can be fired and glazed; paper-clay can be varnished.

One enjoyable project is 'biscuit modelling', in which figures are cut out flat from the strip with a biscuit mould, and decorated with little stripes and pieces of different colours. Unfortunately, superimposed pieces are apt to come loose in the drying if clay is used, and they should be firmly fixed with clay 'slip'.

Plaster moulds

The flat relief such as described above leads on to the making of plaster moulds, which makes possible the mass production of clay or plasticine reliefs. Plasticine is particularly well suited to this, as it is oily and so needs no preparation for use with plaster.

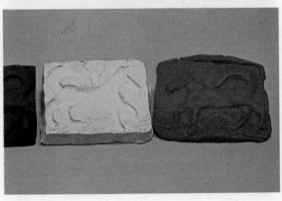

For making the mould the relief is placed on a sheet of glass and surrounded by a frame or well of plasticine. Into this walled enclosure the plaster is poured and allowed to settle and harden. One can recognize the setting process as the plaster becomes warm. With the resulting plaster matrix, as many clay, paper-clay or plasticine impressions can be made as desired.

There are further possibilities with the disc or plaque, for if made of clay or paper-clay it can be coated with 'slip' of another colour. Clay can also be painted with powdered clay that has been liquefied and artificially coloured, see p. 46.

21

To get a durable coating paint only on a damp back-ground. After painting with clay 'slip', the sgraffito technique follows naturally. In this the whole disc, plaque or medallion is coated with 'slip' or with powdered clay and left to dry. Then a pattern is scratched through with a pointed instrument, revealing the differently coloured ground.

Other projects

And now once more back to the ball or sphere. The smallest and simplest objects in this form are beads for a necklace. They are formed by rolling in the fingers and pierced with a knitting needle. Paper-clay can be dried and painted, clay beads fired and glazed. It is obvious that numberless variations are possible with

such beads and necklaces, nor should one confine oneself just to the simple, spherical bead. Imprinting and painting increase the possibilities.

The partially dry but unbaked clay ball can be bored and carved in many interesting artistically interesting ways.

Generally speaking, carving and sandpapering the basic forms which you have made is a rewarding task.

As there are no dogmatic rules on the subject, one can give free rein to one's imagination. The illustration above shows a model that started as a lump of clay clenched in the hand; through cutting and polishing it has taken on a new form. But back again to the sphere. If we take one in both hands and press into it with both thumbs, the result is a primitive form of container — the bowl, which can be pressed out quite thin with the hand.

The best and most successful size is the hand size, and after the sphere they are the first objects which can be made to serve a useful end.

a

24

b

Plasticine is very suitable for play purposes in the early stages, and for training the hand, but one can understand that children would like the things they have made to be lasting. Clay bowls of this sort are best fired at a temperature of 600°C, about 1100°F., after which they can fairly safely be smoothed down with sandpaper if the surface

c

d

has been left too rough in the handling. The bowls illustrated are (a) painted with liquified powdered clay, (b) decorated with sgraffito, (c) glazed and then painted with majolica paints (see p.47). The bowl (d) is of paper-clay; it has been painted inside with tempera and smoothed outside with sandpaper and finally enamelled.

But we must not stick just to little bowls, as one can lapse too easily into a sort of mass production of

ash trays, and this is technically and artistically sterile. One should seek to develop the bowl further, into the hollow sphere, and then, by skilful cutting, into the skeleton ball, and even the double skeleton ball — one inside another.

With the bowl and the tube a wide variety of objects are possible.

Coiled Pottery

Now it is time to talk about coiled pottery, which is a very ancient and simple craft. For this one needs a long, narrow roll of clay, and if possible, one of even thickness throughout. The vessel is formed in a spiral, as the illustration shows. But special care must be taken here that the layers are well coated and joined with the clay 'slip'. It is a good idea with small children to practice first with plasticine. The 'slip' coating alone is not sufficient: layer must be firmly pressed on layer, and the inside of the coils smoothed as evenly as possible. The handle or any other attached part must be carefully worked and joined if it is not to fall off even before the firing.

The coil character of the outside can be left as it is, or it can be smoothed down, in the 'leather

hard' condition by rubbing with a knife blade, or, if allowed to become absolutely dry, by sand-papering. A very useful piece of equipment here is the revolving modelling stand, see p.70.

see p.70.

There are no limits to the forms which the imagination may suggest, nor should one be restricted to bowl and vase shapes.

Finally glazing and painting put the finishing touches on the baked clay models.

Now we can make a start on actual sculpture. Hollow ware has one big advantage over that pressed out from the rough lump – it dries and fires much better, as the walls are thin and even. Thick, solid clay bodies are apt to collapse in the kiln, especially when moisture is trapped in the clay. Another advantage of coiled sculpture is that one needs so much less material, even if experience shows that this method is rather more difficult. Naturally the form is thoroughly smoothed down.

Work on the potter's wheel should logically follow now, but that is far too big a subject for this book.

Free modelling

Up to now we've said nothing about free modelling, by which we do not mean the hand-kneading used by small children, but sculptured figures which involve a mixture of techniques. It is done as illustrated, the parts being joined again. The basic form is usually made in a single piece, superfluous material being cut away and other material being

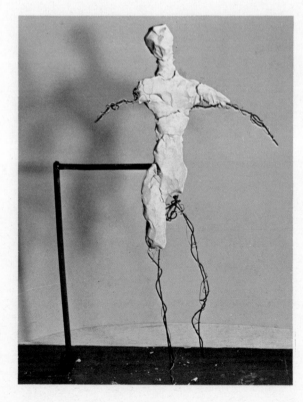

added. With clay, paper-clay or plasticine one can make forms of only a certain size before the model collapses under its own weight. This is a particular problem if there are free-standing arms and legs. Internal or external support is then essential. With plasticine and paper-clay this is no problem. Paper-clay, like clay, dries after a time on the supporting wire, and it is not harmed thereby. It is advisable to provide even small paper-clay figures with a support of wire of thin wooden sticks, for it is not apt to break away from the support. Clay, however, is rather sensitive where internal bracing is concerned. As the moisture dries out of it it shrinks and crumbles and comes away from the support – and all the work put into it is wasted. Clay figures must therefore be kept damp.

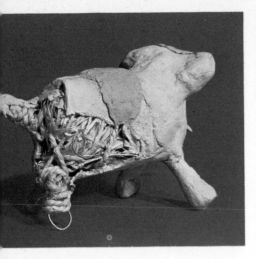

Often the lapse of a day or even more cannot be avoided while working on a piece, so, at the end of each spell, the sculpture should be well wrapped in damp cloths and enclosed in a plastic sheet or bag to prevent evaporation.

Braced figures in plasticine or clay are impermanent; if one wishes to keep the work, one must make a plaster cast (see p.33).

Paper-clay does not collapse from its support, and advantage can be taken of this fact to save material. Paper or cloth balls, wound about with string or wire, can serve as the core of the figure, which will now be covered with a thin coating of paper-clay. Or a string can be wound around a wire support, and then covered.

When one thinks of plastics and schoolwork, puppet heads come at once to mind. Head, hands and feet must be light yet resist hard handling and knocks. There are several ways to achieve this.

The papier-mâché head is an old and well-known form. We start with the cardboard tube for the finger, and on this we build up the rough shape of the head, either by gluing or binding. This basic shape consists of a tightly crumpled paper ball, and around this the glued papier-mâché will be formed and shaped. For drying it, we insert a wooden stick and stand it in the neck of a bottle so it can easily be painted and varnished.

Paper-clay gives results which are just as good, and it is simpler to use (see p.30). This method also has the advantage that finer details are possible than with papier-mâché.

Neither clay or plasticine are of use for puppet heads, but both, and plasticine especially, make possible an interesting technique. Plasticine can be modelled to a fine and delicate degree, and heads, hands and feet can be made from it, though of course, not for actual use. But we can use the plasticine head as the core for an especially light and durable puppet head. We do this by holding the

head securely in a bottleneck, and then covering it with layer upon layer of tissue or crepe paper well soaked in paste or glue. The paper is carefully pressed on so that the covering is uniformly thick overall; it can scarcely be too thick.

When the head is completely dry it is cut in halves with a sharp knife, and the plasticine is easily loosened from the inside. Then the hollow halves are glued together again, and the seam is hidden with gummed paper. The head is allowed to dry again and painted with a neutral colour. Details and features can be added in tempera or water colour and finally varnished. The thickness of the hollow neck can be adjusted by adding strips of gummed paper.

Plastic moulding for advanced pupils

We have already talked about relief moulding, but the form we are now to deal with is rather more difficult and complicated. As our starting point we can use the puppet head again.

We need plaster, a bowl to mix it in, and some thin metal sheet (as from a condensed-milk tin) which can easily be cut with shears, or some thin zinc. From this little squares are cut, and these are stuck around the head, forming a dividing line, and smeared lightly with oil.

Now mix the plaster: fill the bowl three-quarters full with water, adding spoonsful of plaster slowly, allowing it to sink until just a small peak of plaster shows above the surface. Only then start to stir. Into this liquid plaster, which should have a thick but pourable consistency, put a spoonful of red or brown colouring. The purpose of this colour will presently become clear. Coat the head thinly with the plaster, taking care that the dividing layer of metal squares protrudes. This plaster covering should not be thicker than about a third of an inch. When it is hard and firm, go over it with potash water, following this with another, thicker coat of uncoloured plaster. After half an hour or so the plaster will have set. But here a word of caution: use only fresh plaster; stale plaster will not bind but remains spongy.

The metal dividing layer is drawn out, the plaster will not have stuck to the oily surface, and the mould will fall into two halves, from which the plasticine or paper-clay 'positive' or core can be easily removed. The mould is dipped in water and the hollow carefully brushed with soapsuds. It is now ready for the pouring. The two halves are matched together accurately and bound, the split left by the metal strips being filled with plaster, clay or plasticine. The liquid plaster is now poured in, making sure that none seeps through the joint. Now one must be patient, for the plaster must become absolutely hard. It is better to wait two hours rather than one!

After the cord binding is unfastened the plaster mould can be removed, piece by piece, with hammer and chisel. The mould is, of course, destroyed. When the red or brown layer appears, one is warned that immediately under it is the snow-white, easily damaged cast.

If the model is uncomplicated, without awkward projections, it is possible to save the mould; it can be dried, and inside the two halves, a thick layer of clay is kneaded, and the halves then put together, forming a hollow copy of the original solid figure.

In this way it is possible to reproduce relief-decorated vases. The original vase is made as a solid form and then one proceeds as described. The layer of coloured plaster can be omitted if desired, as it is not necessary.

In making vases in this way, care must be taken to see that the walls are of even thickness. After about an hour the vase will free itself from the plaster mould, which will have absorbed much of the moisture from the clay, causing the clay to shrink slightly.

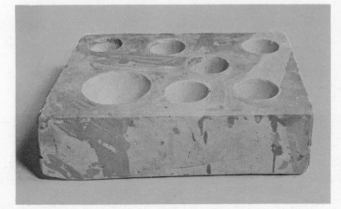

Clay casting

We will discuss the plaster mould a little more, as there is still another method of making hollow shapes. It depends on two basic facts:

1. Dry plaster absorbs water thirstily.

2. Powdered clay, stirred up in water, with a few drops of sodium silicate added, can be poured for casting. (for more details see p.40). Liquid clay holds a great deal of water, which needs to be absorbed, so especially thick plaster moulds are necessary.

The simplest type is the 'beaker casting' in conical moulds. The model is made of solid clay. It is set upside down, the greatest width at the bottom, on a glass slab, and surrounded with a 'box' which is large enough to leave a space of at least an inch between it and the model. This space is filled with plaster, and when this has set the model can be removed. The resulting mould must then dry thoroughly (8-10 days).

Now the liquid clay is poured into the mould till a small heap of the clay is above the level of the mould. The plaster draws the water from the clay, and a fine, dense layer adheres to the inside of the mould. It is clearly seen how the liquid clay gradually disappears as it is poured and repoured. The strength and permanency of the resulting beaker depends on the type of clay used, as well as on the condition of the plaster mould, and in each case this must be verified by experiment

When the clay lining has been built up sufficiently thick, say between an inch and two inches, the surplus clay is poured back into the container. After a while the beaker will dry and become loose from the mould if this is turned upside-down. In the pouring some of the liquid clay will have run over the edge and dried. This should be carefully removed with a knife, for the edge of the beaker must look quite clean. The end result is a beaker with walls of even thickness throughout. One must not be surprised if the beakers are smaller than the original model. If one wishes to make one of a specified size, then the model must be made slightly larger. It is difficult to give the percentage loss in size between the still wet model and the finished, baked article, as each sort of clay shrinks differently, and several times:

1. in the drying and setting.
2. in the firing kiln (up to 600°C. or 1100°F.).
3. in the glazing kiln (from 900°C. or 1650°F.).

Changes in volume due to shrinkage
a. the unbaked, wet original
b. same piece, when dried
c. after firing in the kiln
d. at 1100°C. 1800°F. before vitrification.

The best way to arrive at a safe conclusion is to prepare a clay tablet 2 inches by 4 inches and a third of an inch thick. This will be measured several times: in soft, wet condition; in dried state; and after firings at 600°C. 1100°F., 800°C. 1350°F., 1000°C. 1800°F., and 1100°C. 2000°F.

The process we have just described makes it possible to cast far more complicated vessels, but this, naturally, necessitates far more complicated moulds.

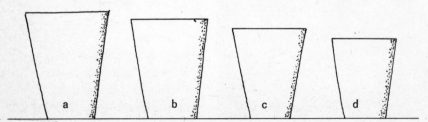

a   b   c   d

The example shown in the illustration is the casting mould of a coffee pot.

Between the kneading of a little ball and the casting of complicated hollow ware lies an immense range of modelling possibilities, of which only the basic technique can be introduced here, and the artistic scope is widened by painting and glazing. It might be mentioned here that broken pieces of glazed pottery can be the basis for coloured mosaic.

Enough has been said about plasticine and paper-clay. Clay pottery is much more difficult, and it is about clay, its preparation and storage, of glazing and firing that we shall speak in the following chapter.

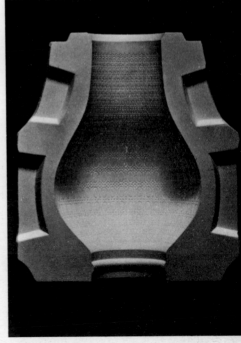

TECHNICAL APPENDIX

All raw materials and kiln equipment mentioned in this chapter, e.g. clay, glazes, clay colouring, firing and glazing colours, fireclay powder, base plates, etc., are obtainable from art-supply stores.

What one should know about pottery

Potter's clay is produced by the weathering and decomposition of rock containing alumina. Pure alumina occurs rarely and for our purpose would be unsuitable. This pure clay, known as kaolin, or porcelain clay, is the raw material of fine porcelain and requires a temperature of 1800 °C. 3300 °F., in the firing.

All clays which are in use in pottery are a mixture of alumina, quartz, mica, feldspar, lime, gypsum and pyrites. Consequently the purifying processes to make different types of clay are varied. First we must differentiate between 'fat' and 'thin' clays; fat clays contain a limited amount of quartz and lime; they are especially plastic and in a moist condition feel 'greasy'. They are particularly suitable for fine modelling. Thin clays contain a larger proportion of lime or quartz (sand), usually of both. From such loamy clays they make bricks. It is not uniformly plastic, crumbles easily and dries out very quickly. Such clays are often found close to mine excavations, on roadsides and in meadows where moles have thrown them up. As children we have made little balls of it. This type of clay can be baked, but if we wish to use it for real pottery it must be prepared.

Preparation of natural clay

The dried and finely ground clay is put into a pail of water and left to stand for about a week, being often stirred in the meantime. The part containing the clay settled, the water is poured off and the clay sludge is passed through a fine sieve. The residue is thrown away.

There should be a large plaster plate (a 'bat'), absolutely dry, of course, and on to or into this the fluid clay is poured. The plaster absorbs the water, leaving a kneadable clay, of better quality than that in its raw state.

Such 'natural' clay must be handled with special care during the firing, and test firings are recommended to see how it behaves.

Most satisfactory and reasonably free of risk are the clays from the traditionally rich pits, which supply them for schools and for the amateur potter. Most of this is 'fat' clay, which is thinned down into various grades by the addition of fireclay powder. Fireclay is finely ground clay already once baked. These artificially thinned clays are the most useful for our purpose and we shall be referring only to this.

Types of clay
Apart from the properties already mentioned, clays are classified according to their colour in the raw and baked states. Roughly speaking there are three sorts with which we constantly meet: the white clay, which in its raw state is grey to white, and is white when fired; the yellow-brown clay, yellow in its raw state, occasionally almost red, and nearly always red when baked (owing to the presence of iron oxide); and the brownish black clay which bakes to a dark brown or almost black, due to the presence of a large proportion of manganese.

Storing the clay
Proper storage cannot be taken too seriously, for stocks are all too quickly spoiled by inefficient handling. Moist, kneadable clay can dry out, powdered clay can become damp and lumpy. Moist clay, ready for use, is best packed in airtight plastic bags, which can be stacked tight for long periods in a wooden box, lined with zinc and fitted with a good, airtight lid. Plastic containers with lids which close tightly serve the same purpose for smaller quantities.

But the safest storage method is as follows: Dig a square hole in the garden, line it with plastic sheeting and lay the clay-filled bags in the hole. Lay another plastic sheet over them and over this a wooden board, on which finally spread a layer of earth. In such a pit clay will keep for years, and actually improve! It is an old potter's method, and a maturing process which makes the clay more kneadable.

Clay powder is usually delivered in paper sacks, and it can be left in these or emptied into a container, the important factor being that the storage must be absolutely dry (in a damp cellar the sacks become moist and rotten and the clay swells).

In order to make the clay kneadable it must be treated with water, and there are two possible ways:

1.   Half fill a bucket with water. The rest is filled up with clay powder, which slowly sinks as the water permeates it. It is important *not* to stir, as this tends to make it lumpy. After a few hours, work it thoroughly by hand. It will often be too wet and in order to render it kneadable it is spread on to a plaster 'bat' which soaks up the surplus water. Sometimes a thick layer of corrugated paper will suffice.. Sprinkling it with dry powder and pummelling it about well by hand will also do the trick, so long as one is not afraid of getting one's hands dirty!

2.   Water and clay powder — the right proportions must be discovered by trial and error with each type of clay — are put together in a strong plastic bag which is securely tied. The soggy mass can now be worked and kneaded without soiling the hands. If the clay is too wet it can be dried out a little on a plaster 'bat' as already described.

How to make 'slip'

The moulding and shaping of clay requires it to be moist and kneadable, but if one wishes to be able to pour it for casting (see p.35) it must be liquefied.

We begin again as when we treated clay powder with water to make kneadable clay. To half a pail of water we add, a little at a time, clay powder, taking care that as it sinks it does not form lumps. After a time the clay is saturated and we allow the mixture to stand for half an hour, then pour off the excess water. Left behind is a soggy, stiff paste, too thick for pouring, and to this we add two spoonsful of bicarbonate of soda, or sodium silicate, the same substance used for preserving eggs. One can normally buy it from a chemist or drugstore. A strange thing now happens: whereas previously no amount of stirring would change the consistency, now, with slow stirring, it changes completely and becomes as liquid as water. This effect is important for casting: it is made with little water, yet it can be poured like water.

One point, by the way! According to the size of the bucket and amount of clay used, one must vary the dose of sodium silicate, and this must be found by experiment. And one thing more! This method does not work with every sort of clay. There are some which are naturally capable of being poured. In case of doubt ask the supplier.

Ready-to-pour 'slip' can be stored in plastic bottles. A good shaking will make it fluid if it has settled after long standing.

Kiln M20/S made by Conrad Naber, Lilienthal near Bremen.

How clay is fired

The perishable clay is transformed by firing or baking into a permanent object, but the firing is the part which gives the most headaches. Nonetheless, it is really not so difficult if one sticks to the basic rules.

1. A modelled or moulded object can never be too dry. The least amount of moisture present will boil with the heat, and the clay will burst.

2. Clay and plaster are the greatest of enemies! Always take care that no crumbs of plaster get into the clay which is to be fired. Pieces of plaster, however small, absorb water and cause the clay to burst ('dunting'). Plaster and clay must always be stored well apart.

3. Never fire more than one sort of clay in the kiln at one time, as different clays have different firing temperatures.

4. Never attempt the first firing and the glazing firing at the same time.

5. Always heat the kiln slowly, then nothing much can be spoiled. Heat at 100°C. 212°F., for 1 hour, a second hour at 200°C. 400°F., then at 600°C. 1100°F.

6. Never be inquisitive and open the kiln during the firing. The kiln covering and the ware being fired do not take kindly to this. Don't open the kiln until it is 'black', that is, when there is no more glow to be seen. This can happen at about 400°C. 750°F. To be safe wait until it is cooled down to 100°C. 212°F.

7. Never stand glazed ware direct on the kiln floor. The glaze becomes fluid at about 1000°C.

1800°F., and it can happen that a mistake can be made in the firing and the kiln reaches a higher temperature. The glaze will then run down the ware like water and stick it to the kiln base, from which it can often be loosened only with hammer and chisel. To avoid this put a thin layer of kaolin on the kiln floor: this doesn't melt until 1800°C. 3300°F., and the glaze will drop on to this and can easily be removed.

After these very elementary precautions, one further one! Pots, figures, etc., are scraped free from glaze on the supports on which

Tripods and triangular supports, 'kiln furniture'.

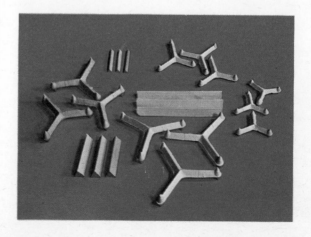

they stand in the kiln. The safest method is to scrape the ware free and then stand it again on porcelain tripods or triangle supports ('kiln furniture').

What happens to the clay in the firing process?

Clay is a mixture of very fine grains and water, which causes the tiny particles to cling together and swell up, and these in conjunction make the clay plastic. This water must be eliminated before firing. If you change your mind about a piece you have made, and decide not to fire it, break it into small pieces and wrap them in a damp cloth and let them really soak. The clay will then be kneadable again a day later.

But even in 'bone-dry' clay some water remains, so-called 'crystal water' which is chemically fixed and not set free till a temperature of 550°C. 1022°F. If the clay is baked, then broken up small and mixed with water, the clay grains do not swell up again: the clay has lost its plasticity.

Now the clay is baked yet more, but it still has no real rigidity and strength. It is still soft and breakable and can be scratched with a fingernail.

From 600°C. 1100°F., upwards the clay solidifies. The tiny fragments melt together and give the whole mass stability.

According to the type of clay it loses in varying measure the property it formerly had of permeability and porosity. The tiny pores close at between 1000°C. 1800°F., and 1300°C. 2375°F., and the clay vitrifies. Some clays do this at only 800°C. 1500°F.

Sometimes the glazing temperature is not much higher than the first ('biscuit') firing temperature. Small figures which are to be kept can be fired at 650°C. 1200°F., and then painted and varnished.

Ware which is to be glazed is fired at 800°C. 1475°F., when it will be firm yet capable of absorbing small amounts of the water important in glazing. Clay figures which are *not* to be glazed can be fired up to 1100°C. 2000°F. After this, glazing can indeed be rather difficult, as the hard-baked ware cannot absorb enough water. So here too, make trial firings.

What must be known about glazing

Glazes are silica combinations similar to glass. There are complex alloys of quartz, a little lead oxide, limespar, soda or potash with a flux such as lead or borax. In the firing chemical action takes place and they melt together to form 'frit', which is ground to a very fine powder and sold to the potter. Glazes have different melting points and it is advisable, when ordering, to ascertain from the manufacturer this point.

The glaze is coated over the 'biscuit' (the pre-glaze firing) to a temperature of 600-800°C. 1100-1375°F., at which temperature the clay loses the last vestiges of moisture. In this condition the clay absorbs moisture from the glaze coating and causes it to adhere.

There are several methods of applying the glaze:

1. The glaze is painted on with a soft, long-haired brush. This is quite good up to a point, but if a uniform and completely unbroken glaze is required it is not the best method.

2. The glaze is poured over the article from a container, and to save the glaze a larger receptacle is put under to catch the surplus. But success with this method needs long practice.

3. The glaze is sprayed on with a spraygun. This will achieve a quicker and more even coating and this method is employed by larger firms. We only mention it here for the sake of completeness. However, it is possible that a skilful amateur will attempt it with success.

Pot and glaze must be dry before the firing. And be careful with greasy fingers! Wherever these touch the clay the glaze will not adhere.

In the glaze firing one should leave it at a temperature of 100°C. 212°F., for half an hour, then the article can be baked up to melting temperature. Keep your curiosity in check and leave the glazed ware to cool for twelve hours. Opening the kiln prematurely and a too-rapid cooling can cause cracks and flaws.

Glazes come in many colours, which are obtained by the addition of metallic oxide to the clear glaze:

Copper oxide	blue-green to green
Chrome oxide	green
Manganese oxide	brown
Cobalt oxide	blue
Sodium silicate	turquoise
Antimony oxide	yellow
Iron oxide	brown to black
Ochre and iron oxide	red
Tin oxide	white
Cobalt-potash silicate	grey

Generally speaking we have to do with only three of the main types out of the many used in manufacture: transparent glaze through which the undercolour can be seen and which has a glossy surface; the opaque glaze; the matt glaze, which is basically an opaque except that it does not gleam but has an even, dull surface.

In all glazing, one thing must be stressed. If the glaze is too thin, then the glaze effect is questionable, and even an opaque glaze will be transparent, or will even not be effective at all. The same glazing will have, at times, a different effect on different days.

For those interested in the craft, it is recommended that before every glazing, tests be made to find out the effects.

A note on powdered, liquefied clay

Powdered clay, liquefied and artificially coloured, can be used to colour a moulded or built-up article. Red clay can be coloured white, blue, green. Like glaze, powdered coloured clay is carefully dissolved in water and passed through a fine sieve. In contrast to glaze, however, it is not poured (or brushed) on to the baked clay, but on moist, raw clay, otherwise it will not adhere.

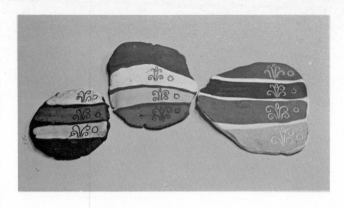

Painting ceramic ware

It has already been mentioned that every clay object can be painted with poster paints or tempera. If such painting is to have permanence, it should be coated with clear varnish. Real ceramic painting is connected with the firing process.

It can be coated, after the biscuit firing, with transparent glaze. The classic painting is achieved by underglaze or on-glaze colouring. Both have their special properties.

On-glaze colour

The on- or over-glaze colour requires that the pot already have a glaze on which the colour can be applied, and the melting point of this, of course, must be lower. If it were otherwise the colour decoration would drown in the molten glaze, and all the work would be wasted.

The melting point generally lies between 700° and 800°C. 1300-1475°F., but it is advisable, when ordering the colour glaze, to make certain on this point.

The colour powder can be ground with water, and some people like to add a little vegetable glue. The powder can also be mixed with good poppyseed oil or oil of cloves if especially delicate painting is attempted.

The underglaze painting is a very difficult form. Whereas the on-glaze colours glaze at low melting points, the former, which are applied to unfired or once-fired pottery, are pure, unmeltable oxides, and must be overcoated with a transparent glaze in order to bring out their colours. This form of decoration is recommended only for the advanced pupil.

Underglaze colour

Supervising the firing temperature

Up to now we've acted on the principle that measurement of the temperature presents no difficulties, and if the kiln has a heat regulator and a thermometer one has little need to worry. But sometimes one cannot afford more than a bare kiln without these valuable accessories.

In this case, and for an accurate temperature measurement, firing cones have been devised. The Fahrenheit temperatures below are exact equivalents of Centigrade temperatures, elsewhere in the text they are only approximate.

Seger Cone no.	Bending point
o12a	870°C. 1598°F.
o11a	900°C. 1652°F.
o10a	925°C. 1697°F.
o9a	940°C. 1724°F.
o8a	965°C. 1769°F.
o7a	975°C. 1787°F.
o6a	995°C. 1823°F.
o5a	1010°C. 1850°F.
o4a	1055°C. 1931°F.
o3a	1070°C. 1958°F.
o2a	1100°C. 2012°F.
o1a	1125°C. 2057°F.
1a	1145°C. 2093°F.
2a	1160°C. 2110°F.

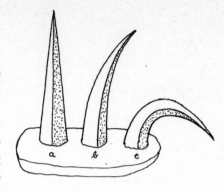

a. Temperature not yet reached.
b. Temperature nearly reached.
c. Temperature reached.

These cones consist of clay that is specially prepared so that they will soften and bend at given temperatures. Check the brand of cone you buy for the exact bending temperature, as these may vary.

When, with the heat, the point of the cone touches the kiln floor, one can be sure that the desired heat has been reached, and if the cone melts and loses its shape it shows that the temperature has been exceeded.

The behaviour of the cone can be watched through the observation hole in the kiln. The safest way is always to use three cones, with different temperatures, e.g. for 900°C. 1652°F., use cones o12a, o11a, o10a. When o12a bends the kiln is almost hot enough. When o11a bends the kiln must be switched off or choked. Cone o10a will show that the temperature is not rising. For it is important that once the kiln reaches 900°C. it remains at that heat for some time.

Finally, there is a great deal more to say about pottery. We have confined ourselves to outlining the basic principles for the layman who is reasonably equipped to begin work. So many discoveries and surprises are involved in firing and glazing that for anyone who takes it up it will never lose its fascination. Each must gain his own experiences and each will discover his own recipes.

The following illustrations show a further selection of form and colour possibilities from the many and diverse fields of modelling and pottery.

'The big weekly market', first
school year. Plasticine.

Crocodile, unglazed and glazed,
girl, 12. Modelled figures, sixth
school year.

50

51

'An enchanted wood', second school year. Plasticine.

Zoo animals, girl, 12. Red clay, baked. The lion and snake are painted with tempera, girl, 13.

An elephant, girl, 13. Grey-black, transparent glaze with white-glazed tusks.

Prehistoric animal. Red clay, baked.

Clay impression (see p.13).

Positive and negative plaster moulds (For technique, see p.21).

Glazed clay relief from negative plaster mould.

Tonal relief, boy, 13. Horse and rider were made from a plaster mould on a plaster tablet. The whole relief is about one to two inches thick.

Free composition in rolled and cut clay slab. Basic motif is the complete or partial bending of the clay into tubes (see p.17).

Elementary basic shapes transformed: cylinders, squares, pyramids, flat strips.

Hollow ware, boy, 14. Not made by coiling, but built up from thin slabs. It can be done, but a lot of care is needed for it. The small cauldron is formed by kneading and passing the clay lump, and stands on three conical legs. For techniques, see p. 16.

Bath-shaped vase, built up from clay strip. The stippled outside effect was done by light jabs with a wooden stick. Green and transparent glaze.

'Stage sets', built up from clay
strip, baked and glazed and
painted with tempera.

Mask hand-modelled from flat
clay slab (left) baked at 600°C.
1100°F. (Right) transparent glossy
glaze, fired at 980°C. 1800°F.

61

Large decorative shape in unglazed clay. Basically flat slab,
curved and shaped by hand and
decorated with scales.

These small dishes are painted
with liquefied powdered clay and
baked. They can be left like this
and varnished. The fire-on transparent glaze, however, brings out
their colour and design. For technique, see pp. 21, 22.

Small dish, painted with Engobe and decorated with sgraffito, finally coated with transparent glaze.

One possibility should not be overlooked. In brickworks one can sometimes buy cheaply, bricks which are of substandard clay. These can be carved and shaped with a knife, though this can be difficult when the sand or lime content is high. The example shown at the top of p.65 is in marly clay with high lime content which before firing is again painted over with manganese clay.

Some days after the firing small pieces of lime sprang out. Known as 'dunting', these are unground, corn-sized grains of unfired lime, which absorb moisture from the atmosphere and burst out. The same thing happens when pieces of plaster get into the clay before firing. The lower illustration on p.65 is of 'handgrip shapes', carved with a knife and sandpapered. Glazing makes them more attractive and durable.

Free-modelled sauceboat, boy, 13.
Red clay, glazed in colour.

Large shallow bowl, free-modelled
from clay lump painted with coloured liquefied clay powder and
covered with transparent glaze.

Two birds, girl, 16. Modelled in solid clay and painted with coloured slip before the firing.
For technique see pp.21, 22.

p.68: Coiled pottery vase, glazed white and afterwards painted with majolica (overglaze).

Above: Simple kneaded bowl with handle, impressed decoration outside, painted with green liquefied clay powder and glazed inside.

Below: Painted bowl, girl, 15. In underglaze colours, later covered with transparent glaze.
For technique see p.46.

A revolving modelling-stand. This appliance is not a substitute for a potter's wheel, but is useful in making coiled pottery, in free-modelling and in painting.

Simple pottery from the wheel. For more elaborate and thin-walled forms much practice is needed. This is the work of an amateur.

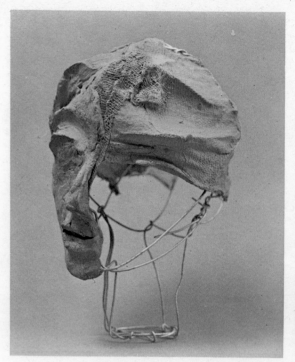

Hollow sculpture in paper-clay with minimal material. The basic frame is of flexible wire, covered with muslin which is soaked and coated with semi-liquid paper-clay. When completely dry the muslin covering is the base for further modelling, (see p.30).

Plasticine puppet head, worked with tissue and crepe paper. Painted in water colour and varnished. For technique, see p.32.

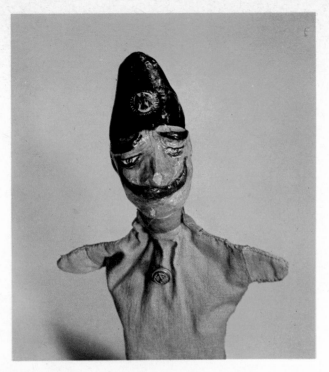

Kiln furniture made by Carl Jager, Hohr-Grenzhausen, Germany. The parts can be assembled in the kiln, and help to make fullest use of limited space.

This head was sculpted with hammer and screwdriver from a clay brick. Here we are on the brink of true sculpture.

Index